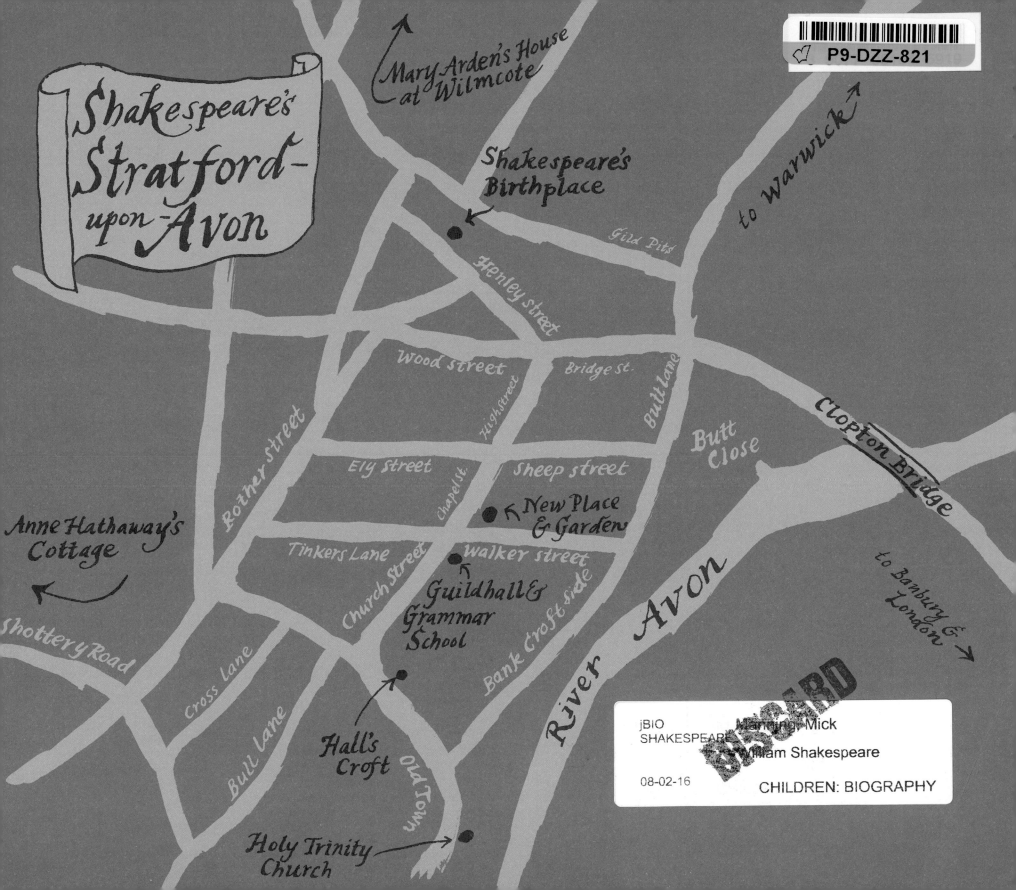

William
Shakespeare

For the indefatigable Do Shaw

The authors and the publishers would
like to thank the Shakespeare Birthplace Trust
and Do Shaw, English teacher, for their
invaluable assistance in checking
the accuracy of this book

JANETTA OTTER-BARRY BOOKS

Text and illustrations copyright © Mick Manning and Brita Granström 2015

First published in Great Britain and in the USA in 2015 by
Frances Lincoln Children's Books,
74-77 White Lion Street,
London N1 9PF

www.franceslincoln.com

A catalogue record for this book is available from the British Library.

ISBN 978-1-84780-345-0

Illustrated with watercolour, pencil and ink

Printed in China

9 8 7 6 5 4 3 2 1

William Shakespeare

Scenes from the life of the world's greatest writer

Mick Manning
&
Brita Granström

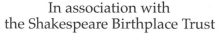

**Frances Lincoln
Children's Books**

In association with
the Shakespeare Birthplace Trust

Shakespeare
birthplace | trust

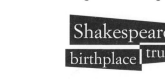

Will is born, 1564

'At first the infant,
mewling and puking in the nurse's arms.'
As You Like It

Welcome to the English market town of Stratford-upon-Avon, over
four hundred and fifty years ago. A baby boy has just been born
to a glove-maker and his wife. In these days, not everything gets
written down and most of what is written down won't survive, so
we don't know everything about this little boy's childhood. But
we do know his name – he is called William Shakespeare and this
book is going to tell you about his remarkable life.

John Shakespeare's fine Tudor house can still be seen today in Stratford-upon-Avon.
It is now open to the public and managed by the Shakespeare Birthplace Trust.

We shall call him William!

WAAHHHH!

Welcome to the world, Will Shakespeare!

... and welcome to my world.

Welcome to the Elizabethan age – a time of struggle between the Protestant and Catholic faiths of Britain. Before Elizabeth I became queen, her half-sister Queen Mary had outlawed the Church of England and prosecuted many Protestants. But by Will's time Elizabeth was queen and the country was Protestant again. Elizabeth prosecuted Catholics, and many executions took place. It was a time of war with Spain, but also a time of new ideas and discoveries in art, science and literature: the age of the Renaissance.

William's mother was called Mary Arden and she came from a well-to-do landowning family. Will's father, John Shakespeare, was a maker of fashionable gloves, and over the years he also held various important positions on the town council: ale-taster, town chamberlain, alderman and eventually bailiff.

Will's schooldays, 1571

'Then, the whining school-boy with his satchel
And shining morning face, creeping like a snail
Unwillingly to school.'
As You Like It

From the age of seven, Will goes to the Grammar School to study alongside other Stratford boys. He learns Maths, English, French, Latin and some Greek – they even do a bit of drama too, acting out the Greek myths and putting on a nativity play at Christmas. Does Will mess about, or does he work hard? (Perhaps a bit of both, because a school desk with 'WS' carved into it can be seen to this day in Will's schoolroom above Stratford Guildhall.) On holidays he helps his father in his workshop or visits his grandparents on their farm, Wilmcote, near the forest of Arden.

Will is the third child, although his two older sisters died when they were babies. He will eventually have five younger brothers and sisters: Gilbert, Joan, Anne, Richard and Mary.

School started early, at 6am. The pupils were from well-off families who could afford an education for their sons. (Girls didn't go to school in those days at all!) The boys studied hard until 5pm, with a 2-hour lunch break. In winter they had to bring their own firewood and candles.

Ugh... not pottage again!

Breakfast was usually pottage, a sort of savoury porridge containing oats, barley, vegetables and sometimes meat.

What a nice shiny-clean face you've got this morning!

Look at you, Will, creeping like a snail!

Will, like other boys in those times, would probably have enjoyed sports such as an early version of football, played with a real pig's bladder blown up to make a ball.

How DARE you carve your initials on a desk!

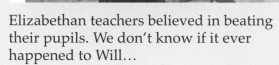

Elizabethan teachers believed in beating their pupils. We don't know if it ever happened to Will…

Will learned Latin and some Greek, discovering the fables of Aesop, the Greek myths and worlds of dangerous adventures, magic and love in the voyages of Odysseus and Ovid's Pyramus and Thisbe.

Recite the Greek alphabet, Master Shakespeare!

Alpha, Beta, Gamma, Delta…

Sir, Will's carved W S on his desk!

I'm going to play Herod the Great!

One of Will's teachers, John Cottam, believed in a system of teaching through drama. We can guess his class probably acted out Greek myths or put on seasonal nativity plays at Christmas. Records survive from other towns that show schools doing exactly that.

Street fairs

'Since once I sat upon a promontory,
And heard a Mermaid on a Dolphin's back.'
A Midsummer Night's Dream

Every year Will looks forward to helping with the 'Mystery' and 'Miracle' plays. He's even been on stage a few times himself. He likes to watch the travelling acrobats and dancing bears but, best of all, he loves the visiting troupes of actors. When they visit any town they must first get a licence to perform from the local bailiff. In Stratford that's Will's dad, so Will sometimes gets to meet his heroes: actors such as the flamboyant Lord Strange's Men. He can't wait to watch their knock-about, slapstick performances on a makeshift stage of planks and beer barrels.

Mystery and Miracle plays were religious pantomimes acted by local trades' guilds. For example the Carpenters' Guild might act out *Noah's Ark*. Will and his father may have taken part in organising and even acting in local shows. When Queen Elizabeth eventually stopped these plays as part of new religious laws, they were sorely missed by everyday people; touring troupes of actors filled the gap.

Actors had a 'bad-boy' reputation as the wild 'rock stars' of their day. To avoid being whipped out of town as travelling beggars, they needed a noble sponsor such as Lord Strange or the Lord Chamberlain. As a boy, Will may have cheered Queen Elizabeth on her way to banquets at Kenilworth Castle. One famous royal performance there included a 'mermaid' riding a 'dolphin'. Will must have heard about it because later, when he became a playwright, he made several references to the story.

Calfskin gloves

'Does he not wear a great round beard like a glover's paring knife?'
The Merry Wives of Windsor

Calfskin gloves are the height of Elizabethan fashion and, at the age of about 15, Will begins to learn his father's business. John has been selling gloves since the 1550s and he is a member of the Craft of Glovers, Leatherworkers and Collarmakers. But John dabbles in other money-making schemes too, and he has got into trouble with the law for selling wool without a licence and for acting as an illegal money-lender. John eventually has to withdraw from the town council, and sells off some of his wife's land around the forest of Arden to meet his debts.

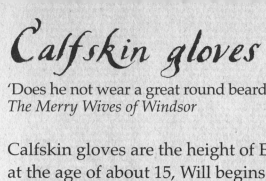

glue pot

That last customer had a great round beard!

brush

calf skin

sheep fleece

newly finished

paring knife

gloves in production

leather purses
and gloves
for sale

scissors and
tools

His beard looked like a
glover's paring knife!

Will's parents may have been secret
Catholics. In an age of anti-Catholicism
this may be another reason why John
withdrew from local office, to keep a
low profile.

John Aubrey, a famous 17th century
historian, was told a story by a
Stratford local about a young Will
pretending to judge and sentence
calves, 'in a high style and making
a speech', before they were to be
slaughtered. But like so much
Shakespeare 'history' it is only hearsay,
not proven fact.

Here we go —
the boss's son
being silly
again!

Mr Calf you are convicted
of High Treason!

In Will's day, England was a dangerous
place. Thieves and cut-throats hid in
woods and wild places, hoping to rob
and murder unwary travellers. But
small crimes could be harshly punished
too. Crowds always gathered to watch
the spectacle of a public whipping
or hanging. It was considered free
entertainment.

Lost years

'Schoolmasters will I keep within my house.'
The Taming of the Shrew

Will's late teens remain a bit of a mystery and there are many ideas about these 'lost years'. They include a Robin-Hood-like legend about a teenage Will fleeing Stratford after poaching deer. Some historians suggest that Will's plays reveal the first-hand experiences of a soldier or a sailor; others see a doctor's apprentice or a solicitor's clerk. More recently there have been suggestions that young Will may have been a teacher at a Lancashire mansion house or a Hampshire grammar school… Lots of exciting ideas, but no one knows for certain… Maybe Will just stayed at home quietly working for his father?

PERHAPS Will was in the army? It was a time of war with Catholic Spain and soldiers were in great demand…

Will's plays show great knowledge of soldiering.

Me? Fight the Spanish?

PERHAPS Will became a teacher? There are countless references to teachers and teaching in Will's plays. In the 17th century, the son of one of Will's acting friends told a historian that he'd heard Will had once been a schoolmaster in the country. But where? Some suggest Lancashire, others a grammar school in Hampshire.

Some say Will was caught poaching (which was a very serious crime) by the squire of a local country estate called Charlecote, and had to flee the district for a while…

You're coming with us, my lad!

It's only John Shakespeare's boy, let him go…

But if so, where did he go and what did he do?

Now, let's try the Greek alphabet again:

Beta…

Alpha…

PERHAPS Will was taken on by a troupe of amateur players, performing dramas and mystery plays in well-to-do homes or local village inns?

PERHAPS Will became a sailor? His plays talk about the sea and sailing a lot... All hands on deck! It was a time of great sea battles, ending with the defeat of the Spanish Armada, a fleet of Spanish warships that attempted to escort an invasion force in 1588.

It looks a long way down!

Dear Sir, regarding your order of 3 pairs of gloves...

... or PERHAPS Will just stayed at home, quietly helping his dad as a clerk? His plays show a knowledge of business and legal matters... and of course at home he could write and make up stories and poems in his free time.

If he did go on stage, Will may have played both men and women's roles, as all female parts were played by males in those days.

Will's later plays certainly show a strong sympathy for amateur actors and provide clever roles for women.

Wotcha say your name was, boy? Shake...shaft?

No sir, it's Shakespeare, sir!

Some people think that after Will Shakespeare left school, he may have become a teacher.

He could have travelled north to Lancashire with his old teacher John Cottam, to work for the family of a rich nobleman called Alexander Hoghton.

Some enthusiasts believe that scribbled notes in the margins of a Hoghton family history book are Will's handwriting.

A William 'Shakeshaft' is mentioned in Mr Hoghton's legal will in which he commends Shakeshaft as well as 'Play clothes' to the care of a friend, Sir Thomas Hesketh (who kept a troupe of actors). But 'Shakeshaft' was a common name in Lancashire, so it could easily have been someone else.

Other ideas include a theory that Shakespeare was a teacher in Titchfield, Hampshire, where his later friend and patron, Sir Henry Wriothesley, owned Titchfield Abbey.

Oh, dearest Will.

Anne Hathaway, 1582

'If music be the food of love, play on;
Give me excess of it...'
Twelfth Night

Whatever Will has been up to, by 1582 he is home in Stratford, and can often be found at a farmhouse just a short walk away, courting a farmer's daughter called Anne Hathaway. Will and Anne quickly marry and move in with Will's parents, and only six months later they have a baby girl they call Susanna. Time passes... Will is probably working with his father, perhaps helping with the paperwork. In the evenings he works on his own poems and dramas. In 1585 Anne has twins: Hamnet and Judith. Then one day Will announces his plans to move to London to try to become an actor and a playwright. His family can't believe it... but Will, promising to visit as often as he can, packs his bag and leaves to the sound of tearful farewells.

Will married Anne Hathaway in November 1582. Susanna was born 6 months later and the twins in 1585. In 1587 a troupe of players called the Queen's Men visited Stratford with some of the best actors of the day, including the famous clown Richard Tarlton. When they got to Stratford they were a man short, as one actor had been killed in a sword fight. Some historians suggest that Will took this man's place and followed the troupe back to London.

John Shakespeare filed over 50 law suits in London so it's not surprising Will writes lots of courtroom scenes and legal language in his plays. He was probably already writing in Stratford, and may have taken rough plays to London to be polished and perfected later. Will may have heard of the local tragedy of Katherine Hamlett, a milkmaid who drowned in the river Avon. If so, perhaps it gave him the idea for a tragic scene in one of his most famous plays: *Hamlet*.

London

'Would I were in an alehouse in London! I would give
all my fame for a pot of ale, and safety.'
Henry V

We're not sure if Will arrives on his own or with a troupe of
actors, but we can guess that London's racket makes his ears ring,
and that its stink makes his nostrils itch. The rickety wooden
houses lean in at precarious angles as he walks along cobbled
streets, slippery with rubbish. After a few nasty accidents, he
soon learns to dodge the smelly chamber-pot slops chucked out
of high bedroom windows. Soon, Will's eyes and ears become
overloaded with new accents, phrases and characters…

London was a lawless place and people carried swords, knives or cudgels for protection. Shakespeare probably made his way into London via the old London Bridge, although many people also crossed the river using ferrymen, the taxi drivers of their day.

These were troubled times! In 1587 Queen Elizabeth executed her Catholic cousin, Mary, Queen of Scots, for treason. By 1588 many others, including the Roman Catholic priest William Hartley, were executed as well. That year a Catholic-backed Spanish invasion fleet, 'The Armada', was defeated by English sea captains including Sir Francis Drake.

Learning his trade

'Speak the speech I pray you, as I pronounced it to you, trippingly on the tongue;'
Hamlet

We can only guess at Will's early days and which troupe he begins with – the Queen's Men perhaps, or maybe Lord Strange's Men? But whichever troupe he joins he must start at the bottom and work his way up. In return for a roof over his head, Will becomes an apprentice, learning his trade amongst the daily playhouse chores, and developing his writing skills too, by helping the troupe's more experienced playwrights patch-up and add new scenes to old plays. But young Will's own ideas soon begin to shine and one of his earliest original performed works is probably *The Taming of the Shrew*. By 1594 he has moved to the Theatre to become a member of the Lord Chamberlain's Men: the best troupe of players in London.

Will may have done some or all of these things:

PLAYING SMALL ROLES and maybe some female parts while he was still young enough – girls were not allowed to act so their parts had to be played by young men.

wigs

white lead make-up

red for lips

underskirts and bum roll

farthing

SWEEPING UP. Theatres were messy places when the crowds went home.

FLYING THE FLAG. The theatre flag flew from the top of the theatre on play days to let everyone know there was going to be a performance.

double and hose

SPECIAL EFFECTS. Making thunder sounds or operating the trapdoor from under the stage.

Today is the day!

DOORMAN AND MONEY TAKER.

Welcome!

STABLE BOY. Holding the horses belonging to wealthy theatre customers.

Hurry up, Will, I'm on stage in five minutes!

DRESSER. Helping to dress the actors in their costumes.

Will! Speak the speech, I pray you, as I pronounced it to you, trippingly on the tongue...

I must remember that...

PATCHING-UP. Helping to write other people's plays and being encouraged to write his own...

I will write a play about a strong woman and call it the Taming of the Shrew.

LEARNING ACTING SKILLS from the actors of the company.

Kill 'em, Harry!

A popular bear-baiting venue in London was the Paris Garden, where famous bears such as Harry Hunks fought vicious dogs. This blood-sport arena was owned by Philip Henslowe, a businessman who also commissioned plays and hired players to perform – often in the same arena. The crowds were rowdy, expecting drama and violence. Sometimes riots would break out if a play didn't satisfy them!

The first purpose-built theatre, called 'the Theatre', had been built by actor-manager James Burbage in 1576, based on the oval shape of bear-baiting arenas such as the Paris Garden. It gave his actors a 'home-ground' – an advantage over their rivals who still relied on touring and inn yards. Other theatres followed, such as the Rose and the Hope, built by Philip Henslowe, and the Swan.

The Upstart Crow

'O, beware, my lord, of jealousy;
It is the green-ey'd monster, which doth mock
The meat it feeds on.'
Othello

Will is now an actor and a pen for hire – he already knows playwrights such as Thomas Kyd, Robert Greene and Christopher Marlowe, who all meet up at the Mermaid Tavern. In fact he has worked with some of them to patch-up a play about Henry VI. Will has been a bit of a magpie. At first, all their writing styles went into his mixing pot, particularly Marlowe's genius with words. But now, using the language he loves, street slang, gang-talk, barmaid's banter, ploughboys' curses, he is beginning to write in his own unmistakable style. Will next writes two plays himself, and *The Two Gentlemen of Verona* and *The Comedy of Errors* get him noticed. His 'boy-wonder' genius is making his rivals green with envy.

Guess who I'm describing. An upstart crow beautified with our feathers... his tyger's heart wrapt in a player's hide... the only Shake-scene in a countrie!

That's a dish fit for the gods.

Very witty, Greene! Are you on fire, Marlowe?

It's tobacco, Mr Kyd – I got it from Sir Walter Raleigh.

A surviving contract for another playwright, Richard Brome, shows he was contracted to write new plays, but also to patch up and add new scenes to older plays. For this he was paid a weekly wage and one day's takings from the theatre. Will may have begun the same way. Parts of *Henry VI* are widely thought to have been written by Shakespeare, working with other writers and learning his trade.

By now Shakespeare may have already acted, alongside a new friend, Ben Jonson, in plays such as Thomas Kyd's *The Spanish Tragedy* or Christopher Marlowe's *Doctor Faustus*. Some of these playwrights may have become friends, others jealous rivals. Robert Greene's famous quote pokes fun at Will, using a misquote from *Henry VI*!

Christopher Marlowe wasn't just a playwright. A friend of the explorer Sir Walter Raleigh, he lived a dangerous double-life as a spy for Sir Francis Walsingham, the Queen's security chief. Marlowe was later murdered in a pub-brawl by a side-kick of Sir Francis's brother Thomas. Perhaps Marlowe found out too much?

In Stratford-upon-Avon, Will has grown up surrounded by hardworking country people. So it's not surprising he writes about them and portrays their lives in many of his plays. This wonderful poem about winter is from Love's Labour's Lost...

Let's go for a frosty winter walk.

When **icicles** hang by the wall. And Dick the shepherd **blows** his nail.

And Tom **bears** logs into the hall. And milk comes **frozen** home in pail...

When blood is nipp'd, and ways be foul, Then nightly sings the staring owl, Tu-who: To-whit! Tu-who!-a merry note, While greasy Joan doth keel the pot...

Say it again!

Is that Aunty Joan, Father?

Winter was well recited: now, let's hear Spring!

When daisies pied and violets blue,

And lady-smocks all silver-white,

And cuckoo-buds of yellow hue...

Love's Labour's Lost is a comedy that dates to around 1594 and was performed at court. By this time Shakespeare didn't just write and act in his plays – he stage-directed them too. Feedback from the performers may have altered and polished his works as time went on.

Visiting home

'When icicles hang by the wall,
And Dick the shepherd blows his nail,'
Love's Labour's Lost

When Will visits home at Christmas to see his family, he's always inspired by watching people at their daily tasks in the frostbitten countryside. Perhaps it reminds him of his own childhood visits to his grandmother's farm. During the last few years in London, several outbreaks of plague as well as food riots forced the theatres to close down for a while. Will spent the time writing and one of his poems, *Venus and Adonis*, will sell more copies in his lifetime than any of his plays. By the time the theatres open again, Will is a shareholder in the Lord Chamberlain's Men and, as their Principal Playwright, is becoming the talk of London town. His new play, *Love's Labour's Lost*, is a comedy that is to be performed at court, and many more plays are to follow....

The Lord Chamberlain's Men toured as far north as Newcastle upon Tyne and possibly further to Berwick-upon-Tweed and Edinburgh. Their patron Henry Carey, Lord Chamberlain since 1585, was already Governor General of Berwick – such an important border town that its defensive town walls were the most expensive construction project of the Elizabethan period. Shakespeare refers to Berwick as 'a faraway place', the farthest point from London, and mentions a con artist, Saunder Simpox and his wife, being whipped back to Berwick 'from whence they came' in *Henry VI Part 2*.

Romeo and Juliet, 1595

'What's in a name? That which we call a rose
By any other name would smell as sweet.'
Romeo and Juliet

Tonight the audience is looking forward to violence and tears as *'a pair of star-crossed lovers take their life'*. The Lord Chamberlain's Men are performing Will's new blockbuster, *Romeo and Juliet*. It stars the greatest actor of the age, Richard Burbage, as Romeo. Will's clever mix of young love, gang culture and swashbuckling street fights spices things up for the rowdy audience. Will's play switches between comedy and tragedy, making the bloodthirsty crowd laugh one minute and weep the next. This tragic love story is going to become one of Will's best-loved plays.

1. At a masked ball one summer's night, a young nobleman called Romeo sees a girl. He approaches her as she takes off her mask for a breather - taking off his own mask. They talk and fall in love...

2. Romeo is a Montague and Juliet is a Capulet, and the two families hate each other. So when Juliet's cousin, Tybalt Capulet, sees them together he goes to find his sword.

6. Later, Romeo's best friends, Mercutio and Benvolio, meet him in town. Romeo begins to tell them what has happened but is interrupted by Tybalt with his gang!

7. But Romeo can't fight them... He is secretly married to Tybalt's cousin Juliet and they are now his family.

11. The friar sends a message to Romeo but it never reaches him. When Romeo hears Juliet has died, he is heartbroken and comes back to Verona. He kills Count Paris outside Juliet's tomb and goes in...

You kiss by the book.

3. Meanwhile, unaware they are from rival families, Romeo and Juliet have fallen head-over-heels in love and they kiss before he flees.

O Romeo, Romeo! Wherefore art thou, Romeo?

4. That night on her balcony Juliet meets Romeo and they arrange to meet again at Friar Laurence's chapel the next day...

But, soft! What light through yonder window breaks? It is the east and Juliet is the sun.

5. Even though they are very young they are secretly married by Friar Laurence, who hopes to bring peace to the bitter feud!

8. Mercutio fights Tybalt instead and when Romeo tries to stop them, Tybalt stabs Mercutio through the heart. Angry Romeo fights Tybalt and kills him...

9. Romeo has killed Juliet's cousin Tybalt! He is then banished from Verona.

10. When Juliet finds out she is going to be forced to marry Count Paris, she tells the friar, who hatches a desperate plan. He gives Juliet a sleeping potion that will make her appear dead. She can then run away in secret to be with Romeo...

Poison, I see, hath been his timeless end.

12. But Romeo doesn't know anything about the plan! He thinks Juliet is really dead... When he gets into the tomb he takes poison to die by Juliet's side.

13. After he dies Juliet wakes up! Everything has gone terribly wrong.

O happy dagger! ...there rust and let me die.

14. Juliet kills herself with Romeo's dagger.

For never was a story of more woe, than this of Juliet and her Romeo.

15. Capulets and Montagues make peace and bury Romeo and Juliet together.

A Midsummer Night's Dream, 1595

'I know a bank where the wild thyme blows,
Where oxlips and the nodding violet grows,'
A Midsummer Night's Dream

Last year, Will was asked to write a play to celebrate a wealthy London wedding and he has invented a romantic comedy about magic and mistaken identity. Tonight the Lord Chamberlain's Men are performing it at the wedding of the Lord Chamberlain's granddaughter, Elizabeth Carey, in front of the bride's godmother, Queen Elizabeth herself! It is called *A Midsummer Night's Dream* and it contains lovers, fairy royalty, elves and sprites, not to mention a comic villager called Bottom, complete with donkey's head. The performance is a delight for the audience and actors alike. Everyone loves it, especially the queen.

Hermia Demetrius Lysander Helena

1. Hermia has refused to marry Demetrius, a spoilt young man chosen for her by her father, as she and Lysander are in love. Helena is in love with Demetrius, yet Demetrius wants his arranged marriage to Hermia! They all end up in the forest on Midsummer's eve.

5. However Puck gives the potion to Lysander by mistake.

6. - and he falls in love with Helena.

7. Now both men are fighting over Helena, who thinks they are teasing her. The men are rude to poor Hermia, who becomes very upset.

9. Bottom and his furry ears are made a fuss of by the queen's fairy servants and amusing scenes follow.

10. Finally Oberon and Titania make friends and Puck sets everything to rights. Lysander returns to loving Hermia and Demetrius remains in love with Helena. So both couples are happy at last.

11. Bottom gets his human head back and thinks it all a strange dream. The players perform their play, the tragedy of Pyramus and Thisbe, and the audience enjoy it, thinking it is a slapstick comedy. Everything ends with Puck's final speech to the audience...

2. Meanwhile the fairies have gathered in the forest. But their king, Oberon, is having a lover's tiff with his queen, Titania.

3. Oberon plays a trick on Titania. As she sleeps, he drips a magic love-potion on her eyes... she will fall in love with the first thing she sees when she awakes.

4. Oberon tries to help the squabbling lovers by ordering Puck to put some of the love potion on Demetrius' eyes, hoping he will fall in love with Helena.

8. At the same time another hilarious story is unfolding... Some amateur actors rehearsing a play in the forest are spotted by mischievous Puck. He uses magic to give the bumbling character Bottom a donkey's head. Titania wakes up, sees Bottom and falls in love with him.

New Place, 1597

'If you prick us, do we not bleed? If you tickle us, do we not laugh?'
The Merchant of Venice

Will's only son, Hamnet, died in 1596, probably from plague. But his daughters survived, and by May 1597 Will has bought the second-biggest house in Stratford for his family and their servants. The gatehouse fronts onto the main street and the family house, stables and servants' quarters are set back in the private walled garden. But Will still misses his son and lives a large part of his life in London. Over the years he buys more properties in both Stratford and London, renting them out as a landlord. Will is not only famous now but very wealthy. Back in London his play, *The Merchant of Venice*, is performed for the first time.

New Place is no longer standing, but archaeological digs give the impression it was a house set back from the street with servants' quarters, stables and various workshops and outbuildings and a large garden. It also had an impressive gatehouse building fronting onto the street.

Will visited home more and more as he got older, and probably wrote some of his most famous plays at New Place.

The master's home for the holidays.

Yes, mistress.

The Theatre had been built by Richard Burbage's father in 1576 on land leased from a rich property owner, Giles Allen. Standing room cost one penny. Upstairs gallery standing room cost two pennies and with a stool, three pennies. There were small boxed-off areas for wealthier customers. But when the lease expired, Allen claimed the Theatre was his and Burbage argued that only the land belonged to Allen, not the building. A legal battle followed until one dark night Burbage and Shakespeare had a better idea…

As You Like It developed from a story called *Rosalynde* by Thomas Lodge. This is a delightful comedy about country life set in the forest of 'Arden'. Will's mother's family name was Arden, and they owned woodland near Stratford. This comedy remains one of Will's most popular plays with audiences. It features some famous quotes such as 'All the world's a stage'.

The Theatre, 1598

'All the world's a stage,
And all the men and women merely players...'
As You Like It

The playhouse where the Lord Chamberlain's Men perform is called the Theatre and it stands on land leased from Giles Allen, a rich London property owner. But now the lease has expired, and Allen claims the Theatre is his! Will and his friends begin legal proceedings, causing the Theatre to close. What happens next is almost like a comedy scene from one of Will's own plays. While Giles Allen is away from London celebrating Christmas at his country mansion, Will, Richard Burbage, fellow actors and friends dismantle the Theatre with the help of a master-carpenter named Peter Street. Then they smuggle away the most useful parts to a riverside warehouse.

The Globe, 1599

'... or may we cram
Within this wooden O the very casques
That did affright the air at Agincourt?'
Henry V

Peter Street is an experienced builder and in the spring of 1599, re-using many bits of the Theatre building, he skilfully erects a new outdoor playhouse for Burbage on the other side of the river from the Theatre. Its roof is open to the sky, and it has a sign outside showing Hercules holding up the world, and its own motto: 'The whole world is a playhouse.' It has a large stage with columns painted like marble, and a canopy decorated with moon and stars. It has carpenters, stagehands and wardrobe keepers. It has masks, jerkins and breeches; tunics, dresses and nightshirts; sheets for ghosts, cloaks for senators, robes for kings. It has a balcony for musicians and a trapdoor for special effects… but best of all, it has William Shakespeare!

A surviving Elizabethan theatre props list gives us an idea of what may have been at the Globe: stools and tables, a bed, a cave, a lion's head and a wooden leg.

Other stage effects included trapdoors for magical appearances and wobble boards for thunder, musical interludes by musicians, torches and bottles of coloured water with candles behind them for atmospheric effects and night scenes.

Henry V, 1598-1599

'Once more unto the breach, dear friends, once more;
Or close the wall up with our English dead!'
Henry V

The Globe is packed to bursting point. Crowds push and jostle, cheer and shout as they watch Will's latest play, *Henry V*. It's a patriotic, boo-hiss crowd-pleaser with Will himself acting as the 'chorus', a commentator who speaks directly to the audience, urging them to use their imagination and travel back to the faraway days of King Henry V's blood-and-guts victory over the French at the Battle of Agincourt.

O villain! thy lips are scarce wiped since thou drunkest last.

1. Previously, in Henry IV, Parts 1 and 2, audiences had witnessed Prince Hal's wild youth, hanging out with petty thieves in the Boar's Head tavern and avoiding responsibility. His mates in the tavern included lovable rogues such as Sir John Falstaff, Pistol, Bardolph, a girl named Doll Tearsheet and the tavern landlady, Mistress Quickly.

2. Now, as King Henry V, he disowns his low-life friends. When a plot to assassinate him is uncovered, he executes the traitors, including a close friend called Scroop. Later, in France, he mercilessly hangs his old soldier-friend Bardolph for looting. Happy-go-lucky Prince Hal has turned into ruthless King Henry, the warrior king!

...Can this cockpit hold the vasty fields of France? Or may we cram within this wooden 'O' the very casques That did affright the air at Agincourt?... Piece out our imperfections with your thoughts...Think when we talk of horses, that you see them!

Once more unto the breach, dear friends.

Casques means helmets!

He's asking us to use our imaginations.

"We're men beached on the sand, hoping to be washed out by the next tide."

3. Before the battle, Henry disguises himself and walks around the camp, talking to his soldiers and hearing their worries - even playing a practical joke on two soldiers. Part of him longs to go back to his carefree days as Prince Hal.

4. Before the Battle of Agincourt, Henry again urges his men to victory with one of Shakespeare's most famous speeches.

"We few, we happy few, we band of brothers;
For he today that sheds his blood with me
Shall be my brother...

And gentlemen in England, now a-bed,
Shall think themselves accursed they were not here,
And hold their manhoods cheap whiles any speaks
That fought with us upon Saint Crispin's day."

"I'm Pistol, Falstaff's old friend."

"And I'm Fluellen, a proud Welshman."

5. The play ends with English victory. But what made Shakespeare's play a huge hit was the way it gave the common people characters they could identify with in their own lives, such as Mistress Quickly, Doll Tearsheet, Pistol, Fluellen and Bardolph. And by showing the way King Henry deserts his old friends such as Falstaff and Bardolph, the play gives a lesson in how power changes people.

"How now, sir John! Be of good cheer."

"God, God, God!"

John Falstaff's drunken antics had been a hoot on-stage in the two plays about Henry IV, and his almost fatherly relationship with young Prince Hal had warmed the hearts of audiences. But when Prince Hal becomes King Henry V and shockingly disowns and humiliates his old friend, even Shakespeare's rowdiest audiences couldn't hold back the tears.

"The world is mine oyster, which I with sword will open!"

News of Falstaff's off-stage death is one of the saddest moments during *Henry V*. In fact Shakespeare wrote a comedy starring Falstaff especially for Queen Elizabeth, because she loved the old rascal so much. He called it *The Merry Wives of Windsor*.

Treason, 1601

'...The play's the thing
Wherein I'll catch the conscience of the king.'
Hamlet

In 1601 the Earl of Essex is beheaded for treason, and Shakespeare's dear friend, the Earl of Southampton, is jailed for being involved. But life goes on for Will and the Lord Chamberlain's Men, and Will's great play, *Hamlet, Prince of Denmark*, an unforgettable combination of murder and treachery, dates to about this time. Will himself plays Hamlet's murdered father, prowling the Globe as a ghost, crying, "Hamlet, revenge!"

HAMLET
Hamlet is a prince of Denmark, sad that his father the King is dead and angry that his mother has quickly remarried his father's brother, Claudius. Then, one wild night, Hamlet meets the ghost of his father. The ghost reveals he was poisoned by his brother Claudius, Hamlet's uncle! It is a huge shock, and in public Hamlet seems to say crazy things, but in private he searches for proof...

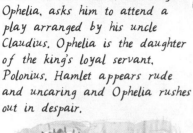

To be, or not to be: that is the question.

1. Hamlet's true love, the Lady Ophelia, asks him to attend a play arranged by his uncle Claudius. Ophelia is the daughter of the king's loyal servant, Polonius. Hamlet appears rude and uncaring and Ophelia rushes out in despair.

2. Hamlet then pays the visiting troupe of players to change their story. He recreates his father's murder onstage and watches his uncle's guilty reaction.

Speak the speech, I pray you, as I pronounced it to you, trippingly on the tongue.

3. Later, in his mother's chambers, Hamlet tries to tell her the truth. But before he can, he hears someone behind a curtain...

4. He stabs through the curtain, thinking it is his uncle... but it is Polonius, spying on them. Hamlet has killed Polonius, the father of Ophelia and Laertes!

5. Claudius sends Hamlet away by sea, planning to have him killed. But Hamlet escapes and meets up with his friend Horatio, who tells him some terrible news...

6. He says that Ophelia, heartbroken at the loss of her father and Hamlet, has lost her mind and drowned in the river while gathering wild flowers.

Alas, poor Yorick. I knew him, Horatio...

7. Attending Ophelia's funeral in the graveyard, Hamlet finds the skull of his old jester.

Another hit. What say you?

8. Back at the castle, Laertes challenges Hamlet to a duel. Claudius has poisoned the wine and Laertes' sword. It scratches Hamlet – a deadly wound! Then Laertes is also scratched with deadly poison.

9. Claudius's guilt becomes obvious as Laertes dies. But then the Queen drinks the poisoned wine. She dies too.

10. Hamlet stabs his treacherous uncle and speaks his final words before he dies...

O, I die, Horatio... The rest is silence.

Good night, sweet prince.

King James 1st, 1603

'Uneasy lies the head that wears a crown.'
King Henry IV, Part 1

When Queen Elizabeth dies peacefully in 1603 the Scottish king, James, inherits the English throne and soon rewards the Lord Chamberlain's Men by renaming them the King's Men. In 1604 Will's new play, *Othello, the Moor of Venice*, is performed at court. But the following year danger strikes, when a group of radicals attempt to blow up the king and his family as they visit parliament. At the last minute, one of the gang, Guy Fawkes, is captured red-handed with the explosives and forced to confess…

We shall rename you the King's Men!

Put out the light and then put out the light.

Othello is the tragic story of a general who marries a beautiful senator's daughter, Desdemona. But his trusted ensign Iago, jealous that Othello has promoted another man, Cassio, fools Othello into thinking virtuous Desdemona has been unfaithful to him with Cassio. The play ends with Othello murdering Desdemona, before Iago is caught.

Now we shall kill the king!

In 1605 the large cellars under the houses of parliament were found to be packed with gunpowder, and some of the plotters turned out to be people known to Shakespeare's family...

1. Three witches are on the edge of a battlefield where, after fierce fighting, Scotland has beaten an invading army. Two generals ride past. One is Macbeth, Thane (Lord) of Glamis and the bravest soldier in King Duncan's army; the other is General Banquo, his old friend.

6. Alone in the dark castle corridor on his way to commit murder, Macbeth sees a ghostly knife that points the way to the king's bedchamber.

7. When he comes back to Lady Macbeth he is carrying two bloody daggers.

Macbeth, 1606

'By the pricking of my thumbs
Something wicked this way comes.'
Macbeth

These are worrying times and Will wonders if he and his family may be suspected as part of the plot against the king. The leader of the gang, Robert Catesby, is the son of an old friend of Will's father, and Will's Stratford neighbour is also implicated. Even Will's local tavern, the Mermaid, is discovered to be a place the gang met. To show King James his loyalty, Will writes a play about treachery and a plot to murder an ancient Scottish king. Will also knows King James is fascinated by witchcraft, so he adds some witches and a surprise ending to the tragedy that makes trees walk and shows the king's ancient Scottish ancestors as heroes. Will calls the play *Macbeth*. The king is so mesmerised by the play he never questions Will's loyalty.

13. Macbeth goes to the witches once more to see if they can set him free. They make a potion for him to foretell the future. The witches warn him to beware of Macduff, Thane of Fife. But they reassure him he will be king until 'Birnam woods shall come to Dunsinane', Macbeth's castle.

2. Macbeth's horse rears in terror when they meet the witches. The witches point at Macbeth and hail him as 'Macbeth, Thane of Cawdor...Macbeth who shall be king'. To Banquo they say, 'Your children shall be kings', and then they vanish in the mist.

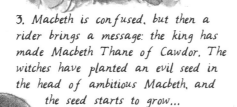

3. Macbeth is confused, but then a rider brings a message: the king has made Macbeth Thane of Cawdor. The witches have planted an evil seed in the head of ambitious Macbeth, and the seed starts to grow...

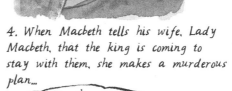

Come, you spirits...and fill me from the crown to the toe top-full of direst cruelty!

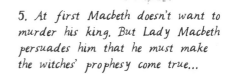

4. When Macbeth tells his wife, Lady Macbeth, that the king is coming to stay with them, she makes a murderous plan...

5. At first Macbeth doesn't want to murder his king. But Lady Macbeth persuades him that he must make the witches' prophesy come true...

8. Lady Macbeth takes the daggers and smears blood over the drugged guards.

9. Next day, the guards are forced to say they committed murder under the orders of King Duncan's son. The innocent sons flee for their lives.

10. Macbeth is crowned but he remembers the witches' prophecy, that his old friend Banquo's descendants will one day be kings.

My lord, his throat is cut...

11. So he hires assassins to murder Banquo and his young son, but Banquo's son, Fleance, escapes.

12. At a banquet Macbeth sees a hooded figure sitting in his chair. But nobody else can see it. When he pulls back the hood, he sees Banquo's ghostly face.

Out, damned spot!

14. When he gets home, Macduff has already fled to England but Macbeth murders Macduff's wife and children...

Life's but a walking shadow.

15. Next, Lady Macbeth goes mad. She walks the castle at night, rubbing at her hands as if she can still see bloodstains. Later she dies of madness.

16. Finally Macduff's army arrives at the castle in a surprise raid using branches cut from Birnam Wood as camouflage. Birnam Wood has walked to Dunsinane.

17. Macbeth is killed by Macduff. Fleance, who has fled to Wales, will one day become the ancestor of the Scottish royal family - and of Shakespeare's benefactor King James.

I will not yield.

Then yield thee, coward.

Twelfth Night and the Sonnets

'Some are born great, some achieve greatness, and some have greatness thrust upon them.'
Twelfth Night

One of Will's best-loved comedies is *Twelfth Night*, a romantic comedy of mistaken identity, first written around 1601 and performed at Candlemas in 1602. It is so popular it is performed in the Christmas season most years. In addition to this old favourite, Will has been producing major new plays too: *King Lear*, *Antony and Cleopatra*, *The Winter's Tale* and many others... Then, in 1609, a collection of 154 poems about love, beauty and the passing of time is published. *Shakespeare's Sonnets* have been written over many years, some perhaps as far back as his courting days with Anne Hathaway, and they will become some of the most famous love poems ever written.

Twelfth Night

1. In the kingdom of Illyria, a nobleman named Orsino pines for the love of beautiful Lady Olivia. She won't marry anyone as she is mourning the death of her brother.

5. There are other amusing characters and subplots involving Feste the cunning clown and Maria, Olivia's maid, who play tricks on Malvolio the prudish gloomy steward, such as telling him to wear yellow stockings to impress Olivia. Olivia just thinks he has gone crazy.

4. Viola becomes Orsino's page and falls in love with him... But when, as Cesario, she is sent to deliver a message to Lady Olivia, Olivia falls in love with Cesario (who is Viola in disguise). It is a love triangle: Orsino loves Olivia, Olivia loves Cesario and Cesario (Viola in disguise) loves Orsino!

8. Later Olivia rescues Sebastian from another fight and asks him to marry her... Sebastian, even though he has never met her before, sees she is rich and attractive and quickly says 'yes'!

9. More confusion follows and some cruel tricks are played by Feste on Malvolio until, in the final scenes, Sebastian and Viola are reunited and all is revealed. At this point Orsino realises he loves Viola and asks her to marry him.

2. Meanwhile a storm washes ashore a young woman named Viola. Viola assumes her twin brother Sebastian, also in the shipwreck, has been drowned.

3. When she hears about Lady Olivia she decides to go and work for her. But because Lady Olivia won't talk to strangers she disguises herself as a man and, calling herself Cesario, she goes to work in the household of Orsino...

I have unclasp'd To thee the book of my secret soul.

6. Meanwhile Viola's twin brother Sebastian has survived the shipwreck and arrives, thinking his sister has drowned in the shipwreck.

He's named Sebastian...

7. Jealous rivals for Olivia's love come to blows as Cesario (Viola) is mistaken for Sebastian, but this gives Viola hope her brother lives.

But that's all one, And we'll strive to please you every day.

10. This delightful seasonal comedy relies on the joke of a woman dressed as a man - made even funnier in Will's time by the fact that in those days women's roles were acted by men. So the full joke is a man playing a woman disguised as a man.

The first known performance of *King Lear* was in 1607 but the play probably existed as early as 1605. At the time many audiences found this play too dark and depressing, as the main character, *King Lear*, descends into madness. However it is now considered to be one of Shakespeare's greatest works.

Many of Shakespeare's sonnets were probably written over many years. Sonnet 145 is believed to have been written for Anne Hathaway and is a pun on her surname::
 "I hate" from hate away she threw,
  And saved my life, saying "not you."
Many others are thought to be for two people: a handsome young man, possibly the Earl of Southampton, and an unknown 'dark lady'.

Allow me to read you part of my Sonnet number 18:
  Shall I compare thee to a summer's day?
  Thou art more lovely and more temperate:
Rough winds do shake the darling buds of May,
And summer's lease hath all too short a date:
  But thy eternal summer shall not fade
 Nor lose possession of that fair thou ow'st;
Nor shall Death brag thou wander'st in his shade,
  When in eternal lines to time thou grow'st:
 So long as men can breathe or eyes can see,
 So long lives this, and this gives life to thee.

Tempest and fire, 1613

'Our revels now are ended. These our actors,
As I foretold you, were all spirits and
Are melted into air, into thin air:'
The Tempest

By about 1609, the King's Men begin to use an indoor
theatre called Blackfriars in bad weather. It has a
roof to keep the weather out and candle lighting, and
Will's last great work, *The Tempest*, is performed here.
But in 1613 disaster strikes the Globe when a theatrical
cannon misfires, setting the thatched roof on fire! One
man's trousers catch light and have to be extinguished
with bottles of beer! But although no one is badly hurt,
the beautiful Globe burns to the ground.

1. On an island a marooned wizard called Prospero raises a magic storm to wreck a ship... so begins The Tempest, a tale of revenge, but with a very happy ending.

Full fathom five thy father lies;
Of his bones are coral made;
Those are pearls that were his eyes;
Nothing of him that doth fade
But doth suffer a sea-change
Into something rich and strange.
Sea-nymphs hourly ring his knell.

Where the bee sucks there suck I; in a cowslip bell I lie.

5. Twelve years earlier Prospero had been the Duke of Milan, but his brother Antonio and the King of Naples had plotted against him. Prospero was put in a little boat with his young daughter and set adrift on the ocean to die. But now he has become a powerful wizard.

Revenge!

6. Next, Prospero calls up a powerful spirit that he has enslaved by magic. Ariel can take any form, a cheeky boy, a unicorn, a hummingbird. Ariel tells him that the shipwrecked crew are scattered around the island and they include his enemies! His brother Antonio is here, as well as the King of Naples, and Ferdinand, the king's son.

7. Prospero plans his revenge, starting with some tricks. Ferdinand is surprised to see lights and hear voices telling him his father is dead. Ferdinand wanders the island...

2. Prospero's gentle daughter, Miranda, runs out of the cave they call home and shouts to him to stop. Before she can ask too many questions Prospero sends her to sleep by magic.

3. Prospero keeps a monster for a slave... Caliban is the son of Sycorax, a long-dead witch who once lived on the island. Using his books of magic, Prospero can command spirits to torment Caliban if he doesn't do his bidding.

4. Poor Caliban isn't very clever, yet he plots revenge. He wants to be king of the island and to take Miranda for his queen.

Caliban!

Our revels now are ended. These our actors, As I foretold you, were all spirits and Are melted into air, into thin air.

Be not afeard: the isle is full of noises, Sounds and sweet airs, that give delight and hurt not.

Here's my hand.

...and mine with my heart in't.

8. Ariel leads Ferdinand on until he meets Miranda, who has been awoken by Prospero. At first she thinks Ferdinand another of her father's magic spirits, but Prospero says he is of flesh and blood just like her. They fall in love, and Prospero plans their love will undo the hatred and treachery.

9. Next, Prospero tells Ariel to find his brother and the king. Ariel plays some tricks on them too, then, in the shape of a talking cloud, leads them to the beach. Here they find all their crew unharmed – and their ship too, floating undamaged and ready to take them home.

10. Ariel then leads them to the mouth of the cave, where they see Ferdinand and Miranda hand in hand. When Prospero appears and confronts his brother, Antonio feels ashamed. 'Let our old hate be ended by this young love,' suggests Prospero, forgiving his enemies. They will now rule Naples together and everyone leaves for the ship.

11. Prospero sets Ariel free and then burns his magic books and his wizard's staff. As the ship sails away, Caliban comes out of hiding and dances for joy – he is king of his island at last...

Ban, ban, Caliban!

William Shakespeare died on 23rd April, 1616. He is buried in Holy Trinity Church, Stratford-upon-Avon. A memorial sculpture and his final words can still be seen: a curse on anyone moving his bones.

> Good frend for Jesvs sake forbeare,
> To digg the dvst encloased heare.
> Bleste be ye man yt spares thes stones,
> And cvrst be he yt moves my bones.

William Shakespeare's plays are largely accepted to be the greatest ever written anywhere in the world, and a life-sized statue of him stands in Westminster Abbey. Yet the First Folio was not published as a collection until 1623, seven years after his death. Many plays which would otherwise have been lost survive in this Folio.

In his introduction to the First Folio, Ben Jonson called Will the 'Sweet swan of Avon'. Will's plays have been on stage ever since and have been made into films, musicals and animations. The English language is peppered with quotes and phrases from the works of William Shakespeare.

Last days, 1616

'We are such stuff as dreams are made on, and our little life is rounded with a sleep.'
The Tempest

The year is now 1616 and Will has retired home to New Place. He still makes business trips to London from Stratford, but he caught a chill a few weeks ago, so mainly he stays at home and keeps warm. When his old friend, Ben Jonson, visits him, Ben says that he is publishing a collection of his own plays called *The Works*, and suggests Will should have his plays published as well. Let's leave Will with Ben, beside the fire, chuckling about days gone-by, days when he mixed with royalty and ruffians, actors and spies – and when he wrote plays and poetry that changed the English language forever.

Glossary:

Bear and bull baiting – a cruel sport involving dogs fighting a bear or bull, often to the death

Catholics – Christians who belong to the Roman Catholic religion, led by the Pope in Rome

Folio – another word for a book or a collection of printed paper sheets

Lease – to rent land or property

Mystery and Miracle Plays – Religious plays staged in towns and villages all over England in Shakespeare's lifetime

Players – another name for actors

Plague – an infectious, deadly disease

Poaching – to hunt deer or animals without permission

Protestant – Christians who rejected the Pope and Roman Catholic traditions

Radicals – people who are in favour of complete political, social or religious reform

Sonnet – a type of short poem originating in Italy in the 13th century

Troupe – a group of actors such as the Lord Chamberlain's Men

References, thanks and inspiration:

Aubrey's Brief Lives, John Aubrey, Penguin, 1972
Being Shakespeare, a live performance by Simon Callow
Shakespeare: the Biography, Peter Ackroyd, Chatto & Windus, 2005
Shakespeare, Anthony Burgess, Jonathan Cape, 1970
Shakespeare's Wife, Dr Germaine Greer, Bloomsbury, 2007
The Globe, a guided tour.
The British Library, London; and also online
Staff at the Shakespeare Birthplace Trust, Stratford-upon-Avon
Ms Sheen, English teacher at Greenhead School, Keighley. 1974-78
Do Shaw, English teacher
Sandra Dods, local historian

Plays by William Shakespeare mentioned in this book are:

Comedies
All's Well that Ends Well, 1604-1605
As You Like It, 1599-1600
The Comedy of Errors, 1594
Love's Labour's Lost, 1594-1595
The Merchant of Venice, 1596-1597
The Merry Wives of Windsor, 1597-1598
A Midsummer Night's Dream, 1595
Much Ado About Nothing, 1598
The Taming of the Shrew, 1590-1591
The Tempest, 1611
The Two Gentlemen of Verona, 1590-1591
Twelfth Night, 1600-1601
The Winter's Tale, 1609

Histories
Henry IV, Part 1, 1596-1597
Henry IV, Part 2, 1597-1598
Henry V, 1598-1599
Henry VI, Part 1, 1592
Henry VI, Part 2, 1591
Henry VI, Part 3, 1591

Tragedies
Antony and Cleopatra, 1606
Hamlet, 1600-1601
Julius Caesar, 1599
King Lear, 1605-1606
Macbeth, 1606
Othello, 1603-1604
Romeo and Juliet, 1595

Poetry

The Sonnets, 1582-1602

The First Folio:

The First Folio was the first true, collected edition of William Shakespeare's plays. It contained 36 of his plays and was published in 1623, seven years after his death. Two of his friends, John Heminges and Henry Condell, supervised the printing, and without their hard work some of Will's plays might have been lost forever. The plays were divided into comedies, histories and tragedies and have been classified this way ever since. Ben Jonson wrote a poem in the First Folio, as a memorial to his old friend:

Sweet Swan of Avon! What a sight it were
To see thee in our waters yet appear,
And make those flights upon the bankes of Thames
That so did take Eliza and our James!

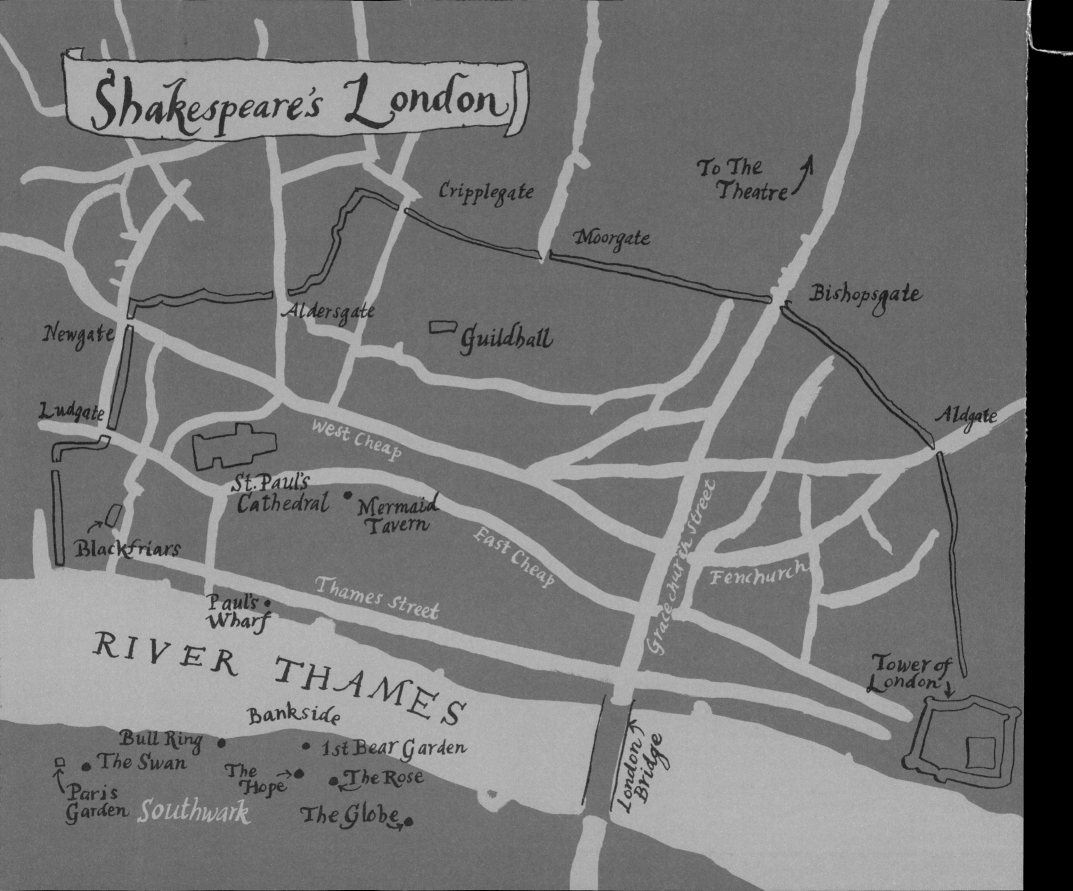